What the Wind Can Do

Written by Lucy Smith

Have you been outside on a windy day?

You cannot see the wind but you can feel it and see what it can do.

You can fly a kite to see how the wind lifts it into the air.

What happens to the kite when the wind dies down?

The wind can be soft and light. It can
make grasses sway and flags flutter.

Gulls glide on the wind.

The wind can be strong and wild too.
Sometimes the wind is so strong it can
uproot big trees!

A strong gust of wind can toss light things left outside into the air.

This is a sailboat that travels across the water.

When the wind fills the sail, it makes the boat go.

The power of the wind can help us in lots of ways. This is a windmill.

inside the windmill

The wind makes the blades turn.
Windmills can grind wheat.

This is a wind farm. You can see wind farms in the sea or on top of hills where it is windy.

blades

turbine

Wind turns the blades on the turbines.
When they turn, power is made. That
power can be made into heat and light.

Wind is a clean way to make power, which is good for us ... and for the planet!